T. C. JUPP

Rich Man, Poor Man

macmillan
education

Macmillan Readers is a series of engaging narrative texts designed to stimulate learners while enhancing their language skills, building literacy and boosting reading confidence. Through captivating stories and fascinating cultural themes, learners will explore a diversity of scenarios that foster vocabulary expansion, comprehension skills and a lifelong love of reading.

The right reader at every stage
Tailored to each learner's stage of language proficiency, our six levels feature text adapted to match the skill level. With controlled vocabulary and grammar, learners can read freely and immerse themselves in the story. When more challenging words are introduced, either the text will provide sufficient context to aid understanding or a full explanation will be provided in the Glossary.

Readers for all, anywhere, anytime
Macmillan Readers are perfect for shared, guided and independent reading. Whether in traditional print, immersive audio or the convenient eBook, Macmillan Readers are equally effective for in-class activities, paired discussions or solo reading at home or on the move.

Reading for pleasure, knowledge and well-being
Regular reading and reading for pleasure:
- increases reading confidence, benefiting all literacy skills, not just reading.
- reinforces and enriches vocabulary, providing a variety of contexts.
- expands general knowledge.
- supports concentration, inner reflection and well-being.

Macmillan Readers will inspire a love for reading in English while nurturing essential language skills. Unlock new worlds, expand horizons and embark on an adventure in English!

(NOTE: While the content of Macmillan Readers is evaluated for age suitability, we kindly remind parents and teachers that they are ultimately responsible for determining whether a particular book is appropriate for their child or student.)

Contents

1

A Letter for Adam

One day a postman came to my village. The postman brought me a letter from my son, Saul.

'Is your name Adam?' the postman asked.

'Yes,' I said.

'I've got a letter for you.' The postman read the envelope: 'Adam of the village of Minta.'

'A letter for me. Who is it from?' I asked.

The postman looked at the envelope again. 'From Saul,' he said. He gave me the letter and walked away.

'Martha, Martha,' I called to my wife. 'Come here. We have a letter from our son, Saul.'

Martha came out and looked at the letter. She was excited but she was also worried.

'A letter from Saul,' she said. 'Is he alive and well? I'm going to find the school teacher. He can read the letter.'

There was no school fifty years ago. So I cannot read or write. I live in a small village. The only work is farming. My only son, Saul, left the village two years ago and my three daughters are married. Saul is making a lot of money in a foreign country.

Martha and the school teacher came back. A lot of other people came. Everyone wanted to hear my letter. The school teacher opened the envelope and read the letter.

> 20 Taylor Street,
> London E19,
> England.
> 16 March
>
> Dear Father,
>
> I am living in London. I have a job in a factory. The work is very hard. I often work at night. But the pay is good.
>
> I am well and I live with people from my country.
>
> I am sending you £100 in this letter. This is for you and my mother.
>
> Love to you and mother,
> Saul

'One hundred pounds!' I said to the school teacher. 'You're wrong. It's a mistake.'

'No', the school teacher said. 'I'm not wrong. It's not a mistake. Here is the money.' And he gave me a piece of paper.

'What is this?' I asked.

'A money order,' the school teacher said. 'Go to Darpur. Take this money order to the Post Office in Darpur. The money order is worth one hundred pounds. The Post Office official will give you the money.'

'One hundred pounds!' I said again.

Everyone laughed and said, 'Adam, you are a rich man. You can buy many things for your farm and for your house.'

'And I can buy some good food and drink in Darpur. I am going to give a party for you all,' I told my friends.

Martha said, 'Saul is a good son.'

That evening, the village people talked about the money order and my money. Martha and I also talked about the money. We needed many things for the farm.

2

Adam Goes to Darpur

The next morning I got up very early. It was dark and everyone was asleep. But I was going to Darpur.

I washed and dressed carefully. I put on my best clothes and I carried my best stick. I put the money order carefully in my pocket and I said goodbye to Martha.

I walked ten miles to the main road. I sat down at the main road and ate my breakfast.

I waited for the bus. I waited for two hours. Then the bus came and I got on.

It is a long way to Darpur. The bus takes three hours. I arrived in Darpur and walked to the Post Office immediately.

I do not often go to Darpur. I only know the market, and one shop. This is the shop of Rick. I buy things for my farm from Rick.

There were a lot of people in the Post Office. I asked about money orders. A man showed me the queue. There was a long line of people and I waited at the back.

MONEY
ORDERS

Finally it was my turn; I was at the front of the queue. But the official did not serve me.

'Excuse me,' I said. 'It's my turn. I'm next.'

'You are next? Old man, I'm very busy,' the official said. 'Look at my papers. Look at all these people. I am very busy. And you must wait.'

So I waited. Finally the official looked at me.

'What do you want?' he asked.

I gave him my money order. 'This is my money order for one hundred pounds,' I replied.

The official held out his hand. 'Identity Card,' he said.

'Excuse me. I don't understand,' I replied.

'Your Identity Card,' the official said again. 'Give me your Identity Card.'

'What is an Identity Card?' I asked.

'I can't give you any money for this money order. First I must see your Identity Card. Your Identity Card gives your name and your address. Your Identity Card describes you. There is a photograph of you in your Identity Card. I don't know you. Who are you?' The official was a little angry.

But I was also angry. 'Who am I?' I said. 'Everyone knows me. I am Adam of the village of Minta. I haven't got an Identity Card and I don't need an Identity Card.'

'Old man, I'm very busy and you're very stupid,' the official said. 'Who are you? Where is Minta?'

'Give me my money. Give me my one hundred pounds,' I said.

The official looked angry and said, 'Show me your Identity Card. I don't know you.'

The official gave back my money order and he turned away.

'Where can I buy an Identity Card?' I asked the official. He did not speak to me. He did not answer.

'Go to the Ministry of the Interior,' a man said. He was standing in the queue. And he told me the way.

An Identity Card

I walked to the Ministry of the Interior. I waited in another queue. I spoke to another official. I asked for an Identity Card.

'Fill in this application form,' the official said. 'And bring the form and three photographs of yourself and two pounds. Come back tomorrow.'

'Tomorrow?' I said. 'Can I have an Identity Card today, please? I live in Minta. I live five hours' journey from Darpur. I'm an old man.'

'Yes, come back tomorrow.' And the official turned away.

I walked away from the Ministry of the Interior. I walked to the market. At the market I looked at everyone. I was looking for a man from my village. But I could not find a villager. So then I walked to the shop of Rick. I spoke to Rick.

'I want an Identity Card,' I told him. 'But I need three photographs of myself.'

'I see. You need some photographs.' And he showed me the way to a photographer.

I found the house. The photographer was asleep but he came to me quickly. The man's clothes were dirty and he looked tired.

'I need an Identity Card,' I said. 'I want three photographs of myself.'

'Yes, you want three photographs of yourself,' the photographer replied. 'And I take very good photographs. Come and see my camera.'

We walked into his room. In the middle of the room was a large camera.

'This is the best camera in Darpur. This camera is very, very good,' the photographer said proudly.

'I've never seen a camera,' I said. 'I don't know about cameras. Hurry up and take a photograph of me.'

'Please do not hurry me, old man,' the photographer said. 'I am an artist.' And he gave me a mirror and a comb.

'I don't want a mirror, I don't want a comb. Please take my photograph. I'm going to Minta this afternoon. And I'm in a hurry,' I said.

'Yes,' he said. 'But first the price. This is the best camera in Darpur and I'm the best photographer. Three photographs will cost you two pounds fifty.'

'Two pounds fifty!' And I laughed.

'Two pounds fifty – and pay me now please,' the photographer answered.

I did not know the price of photographs. What could I do? Then the photographer said, 'You are an old man. For you, the price is two pounds.'

So I gave him the money and he took the photographs. 'Come back tomorrow morning,' he said.

'I want my three photographs now, immediately,' I said.

'Don't be stupid,' the photographer said. 'Photographs take twenty-four hours. Come back tomorrow.'

What could I do? So I said, 'Yes. Tomorrow morning.'

'Good,' said the photographer. 'Now go. I have a lot of work. I'm very busy.'

I went back to the bus station. I sat on the bus for three hours. I walked ten miles back to my village.

It was night time and I was very tired. Martha and my friends were waiting for me. 'Where is the money?' Martha asked.

'I have no money. I cannot change the money order. First I must have an Identity Card.' And I told Martha everything.

'Tomorrow I am going to Darpur again,' I said. Then I did not talk again. I was very tired and it was late at night. I lay on my bed and I slept.

4

No Photographs

I woke up late the next morning. The sun was already high. I did not walk to the main road and catch a bus. All the buses go to Darpur early in the morning.

So I stayed at home on Wednesday. I was still very tired. I rested and talked to the villagers about the money order. I told them about the Identity Card and the photographer.

The school teacher said, 'Yes, the official is correct. In a Post Office, you always show your Identity Card.'

The school teacher filled in my application form for an Identity Card.

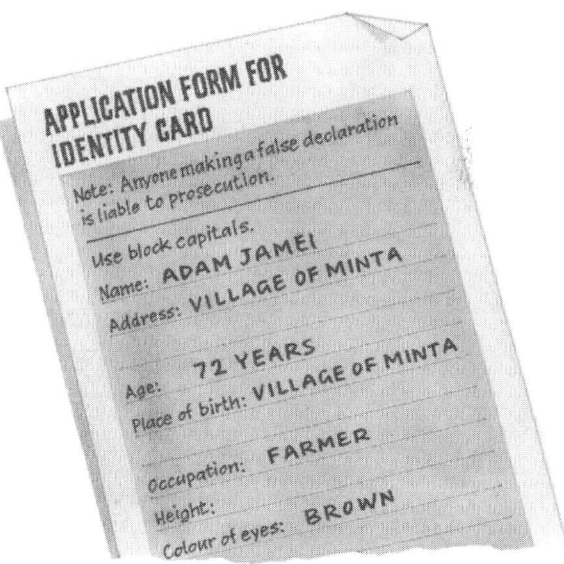

On Thursday I travelled to Darpur again. I walked to the main road and I caught a bus, In Darpur, I walked to the house of the photographer.

I knocked on the door of the house. No one came to the door. I knocked again loudly with my stick. A woman opened the door.

'Who are you? What do you want?' she asked.

'Can I have my photographs, please?' I said.

'Your photographs? I have no photographs,' the woman replied.

'I came here on Tuesday. Where is the photographer?' I asked.

'He's out. He's not here.' And the woman closed the door.

I shouted at her, 'I'm waiting here for him.'

After a long time the photographer came back. He looked tired and he smelt of beer.

'Give me my photographs,' I said. 'I have waited a long time for you.'

The photographer looked at me and said, 'I don't know you, old man. What photographs are you talking about?'

'My three photographs for my Identity Card. I paid you two pounds for them on Tuesday. Give me my photographs immediately or my money.'

'Your photographs? Your money? What are you talking about?' the photographer said. 'Show me the paper. Show me the receipt for your money.'

'My receipt?' I asked.

'Yes. Where is your receipt?' the photographer asked.

'You didn't give me a receipt,' I shouted. 'Give me my photographs or my money immediately.' And I hit the photographer hard with my stick. I am old, but I am still strong.

The photographer fell on the ground. He shouted, 'Help! Help! This old man is killing me.' And I hit him hard again.

Lots of people ran out of their houses. I hit the photographer again and two men held me. I could not get away from the two men.

The photographer was very angry and I was very angry. Lots of people were shouting.

Then a policeman came. The photographer shouted to the policeman, 'This old man hit me three times with his stick. He's a thief and a murderer. He wants my money.'

The policeman held my arm and said, 'Come with me to the police station.' I did not say anything. We walked to the police station.

At the police station, the policeman asked me, 'Did you hit that man three times?'

'Yes,' I said, 'he didn't give me my photographs.'

'Show me your Identity Card,' said the policeman.

'I am Adam of Minta village,' I replied, 'and I haven't got an Identity Card.'

'Old man,' said the policeman. 'Go back to your village. Don't come here and fight. Keep out of Darpur.' And he pushed me into the street.

I went back to my village. I was tired and angry.

5

Adam Changes His Money Order

Next day I told my story to all the villagers. The villagers were angry. Martha was very unhappy.

She said, 'Saul is working very hard. He is sending money and we can't have the money. What are we going to do?'

I did not know. Then in the evening the school teacher came to my house again.

'Adam. Perhaps I can help you,' the school teacher said. 'Here is a letter to Mr Sheth.'

'Mr Sheth?' I said, 'Who is he?'

'He's an important man in Darpur and he's a friend of my wife's cousin,' replied the school teacher. 'This letter is to Mr Sheth. The letter is about your money order. Perhaps he can help you.'

I took the letter and thanked the school teacher.

So I travelled to Darpur again on Saturday, for the third time. After a long time, I found Mr Sheth's house. The door was opened by a tall man.

'Can I see Mr Sheth?' I asked.

'And who are you?' the tall man asked.

'I have a letter for Mr Sheth,' I replied.

'I see. Can I have the letter, please?' And the tall man held out his hand.

'The letter is here,' I said. And I took the letter out of my pocket. 'But I must see Mr Sheth.'

'Many people want to see Mr Sheth,' the tall man told me. 'He is a very busy man and a very important

man. Mr Sheth is not here at the moment. But give me your letter, and Mr Sheth will read it later.'

I gave the tall man the letter. Then I waited. Later, a large black car came and a man went into the house. A long time later, the tall man opened the door again.

'Come in now, please, and follow me,' he said.

I followed the tall man. We went into a large room with fine carpets and big chairs. Another man was in the room. He was drinking.

'This is Mr Sheth,' said the tall man.

'I am Adam of Minta village,' I replied.

'Yes, I know,' said Mr Sheth. 'Thank you for the letter. I hope I can help you. I like to help people. Please, sit down.' Mr Sheth smiled. His clothes were new and smart.

'Thank you,' I said.

'Can I see the money order, please?' Mr Sheth asked.

I took the money order out of my pocket. By now, the money order was dirty and looked very old. I gave it to Mr Sheth.

'This money order is for one hundred pounds,' I said. 'My son sent it from a foreign country.'

Mr Sheth unfolded the money order and looked at it. 'You can't change this money order,' he said. 'This money order is not worth one hundred pounds. This money order is worth nothing.'

'Worth nothing! Worthless?' I asked.

Then Mr Sheth looked at the money order again. 'Yes, worthless. Your son does not understand about money orders. This money order is not correct for our country,' Mr Sheth said. Then he looked at the money order again and said, 'And this money order is also old. It is out-of-date.'

I said nothing. Mr Sheth gave me the money order back.

Then Mr Sheth smiled and said, 'I am very sorry. You are an old man. You came a long way from your village. What can I give you to eat and drink?'

I was not hungry. But Mr Sheth went out of the room. Then he brought me some coffee and some cakes. I drank my coffee.

'Old man,' said Mr Sheth, 'I like to help people. I am a rich man. Give me your money order.'

I gave my money order to Mr Sheth. 'Yes, this money order is worthless,' he said again. 'But I am going to help you. I am going to change this money order for you. I am going to give you some money.'

Mr Sheth went out of the room. I felt very happy again. After a few minutes, the tall man came into the room. He gave me an envelope. 'This is from Mr Sheth. You can go now,' the tall man said.

I went out of the house. I walked along the road to the bus station. I opened the envelope and I took out my money. I counted the money. It was ten pounds. I thought about my only son, Saul.

My son, Saul, had sent me a money order for one hundred pounds. Mr Sheth had given me ten pounds. I felt old and I felt poor again.

Exercises

Multiple Choice 1

Tick the best answer.

1 What is in the picture?

a ☐ Cash.

b ☑ A money order.

c ☐ A cheque.

2 Who sent it?

a ☐ Adam.

b ☐ Minta.

c ☐ Saul.

3 How much is it for?

a ☐ £100 (pounds).

b ☐ $100 (dollars).

c ☐ ¥100 (yen).

4 Which country is it from?

a ☐ The UK.

b ☐ The USA.

c ☐ The UAE.

5 When do you think this story happened?

a ☐ 1800-1899.

b ☐ 1900-1999.

c ☐ 2000-2099.

Making Sentences 1

Match the two parts of each sentence.

1 The postman brought a letter from   farm and for your house.'

2 'You can buy many things for your   were waiting for me.

3 I can't give you any money   my son Saul.

4 In the middle of the room   form for an Identity Card.

5 Martha and my friends   out of their houses.

6 The school teacher filled in my application   for this money order.

7 Lots of people ran   Mr Sheth's house.

8 After a long time, I found   was a large camera.

9 By now, the money order was   dirty and looked very old.

Multiple Choice 2

Tick the correct statement.

1 a ☐ The school teacher told Adam to take the money order to the Library.

   b ☐ The school teacher told Adam to take the money order to the Police Station.

   c ☑ The school teacher told Adam to take the money order to the Main Post Office.

2 a ☐ There were lots of people in the Post Office.
  b ☐ There was nobody in the Post Office.
  c ☐ There were a few people in the Post Office.

3 a ☐ The official in the Post Office was very polite.
  b ☐ The official in the Post Office wasn't very busy.
  c ☐ The official in the Post Office was very rude.

4 a ☐ Adam took the bus to the Ministry of the Interior.
  b ☐ Adam walked to the Ministry of the Interior.
  c ☐ Adam took a taxi to the Ministry of the Interior.

5 a ☐ The photographer said that photographs took twenty-four hours.
  b ☐ The photographer said that photographs took two days.
  c ☐ The photographer said that photographs took two hours.

6 a ☐ A policeman filled in Adam's application form for an Identity Card.
  b ☐ The Post Office official filled in Adam's application form for an Identity Card.
  c ☐ The teacher filled in Adam's application form for an Identity Card.

7 a ☐ Adam was strong and still young.
  b ☐ Adam was old and still strong.
  c ☐ Adam was old and weak.

8 a ☐ Adam had to wait to see Mr Sheth.
  b ☐ Adam saw Mr Sheth straightaway.
  c ☐ Adam didn't see Mr Sheth.

9 a ☐ Adam got all of his money for the money order.
  b ☐ Adam got none of his money for the money order.
  c ☐ Adam got some of his money for the money order.

Making Sentences 2

Write questions for the answers.

1 *Who brought the letter to Adam's house?*

The postman brought the letter to Adam's house.

2 *Where*

Adam lived in the village of Minta.

3 *Where*

Adam's son worked in London.

4 *What*

Adam's son sent a letter and a money order.

5 *Why*

Adam couldn't read the letter because he did not know how to read and write.

6 *Who*

The school teacher read the letter for him.

7 *Where*

Adam went to Darpur.

8 *Why*

Adam couldn't get cash for the money order because he didn't have an Identity Card.

9 *Why*

He went to the Ministry of the Interior to apply for an Identity Card.

10 *What*

He needed three photos from the photographer.

Pronunciation 1

Circle the word with the same vowel sound.

1	**comb**	bomb	(home)	tomb	room
2	**fly**	pay	pet	pea	high
3	**feet**	hear	seat	fight	set
4	**come**	sum	comb	corn	dam
5	**word**	sure	board	wear	heard
6	**part**	heart	port	shirt	pierce
7	**pay**	boy	buy	weigh	see
8	**weight**	height	art	heat	date
9	**long**	tongue	song	rang	bring
10	**might**	way	piece	price	sauce

Pronunciation 2

Underline the stressed syllable.

1	photo<u>graph</u>ic	2	village
3	envelope	4	letter
5	excited	6	worried
7	factory	8	official
9	identity	10	application
11	journey	12	market

Words From The Story 1

Write each word or phrase from the box next to the correct meaning.

> money order   receipt   photographer   village   postman
> envelope   worried   factory   pay   excited

1 A piece of paper that shows you
paid money for something
receipt
....

2 A person who takes still pictures
using a camera
....

3 A small place where people live –
smaller than a town
....

4 A man whose job is to take letters to
people's houses
....

5 The outside cover of a letter – the part
where you write the name and address
of the person the letter is for
....

6 Not calm – very happy, very interested, eager   ....

7 Feeling that something bad will happen
or has happened
....

8 A place where things are made or
manufactured
....

9 Money you earn for a job   ....

10 A paper that is worth money – it is
usually cashed at a post office or a bank   ....

Story Outline 1

Complete the gaps. Use each word in the box once.

> have   brought   _came_   saw   was   working
> knew   called   ask   said   read   do

The postman [1] ....*came*........ to Adam's house. He [2] ....
a letter. Adam could not [3]........................., but he
[4]........................ a strange stamp on the envelope. The letter
[5]............................. from another country. His son was [6]..............................
in a foreign land, so Adam [7]................................. that the letter was
from Saul.

Adam [8]................................ his wife. 'Martha, we
[9]................................. a letter from our son Saul. What shall we
[10]................................. with it?'

'We can [11]................................ the village school teacher to read the
letter,' [12]................................ Martha.

Story Outline 2

Complete the gaps. You must use some of the words in the box more than once.

> a   an   the   this   that

There was [13]......................... letter inside [14].......................... envelope.
There was also [15].......................... paper with foreign writing.
'It is [16].......................... money order,' said [17].......................... school
teacher. 'Take [18].............................. money order to Darpur. Go to
[19].............................. main Post Office. [20]...................................
official will give you cash for [21]................................. money order.'

'How much is it worth?' asked Martha.

'One hundred English pounds,' said [22]............................... teacher.
[23]'............................... is about half [24]............................... million libraat.'

Adam earned half [25]............................... million libraat in half [26]............................... year. It was [27]............................... great deal of money.

Multiple Choice 3

Tick the best answer.

1 How did the photographer cheat Adam?
a ☐ He did not take his photo.
b ☐ He did not give him a receipt.
c ☐ He told him to come back the next day.
d ☐ He drank beer all day.

2 What did the police tell Adam?
a ☐ To get an Identity Card.
b ☐ To go to the Ministry of the Interior.
c ☐ To go to the Post Office.
d ☐ To go home and stay out of Darpur.

3 Who was Mr Sheth?
a ☐ The governor of Darpur.
b ☐ The husband of the school teacher's sister.
c ☐ A foreign businessman.
d ☐ An important man.

4 What does *out of date* mean?
a ☐ Expired.
b ☐ Valid.
c ☐ Punctual.
d ☐ Late.

Macmillan Education Limited
4 Crinan Street
London N1 9XW

Companies and representatives throughout the world

Macmillan Readers Beginner Level Rich Man, Poor Man
ISBN: 978-1-035-15386-2
Macmillan Readers Beginner Level Rich Man, Poor Man with
eBook and Resources
ISBN: 978-1-035-15941-3

This edition first published 2005
This edition published 2024

Illustrated by Michael Charlton
Cover photograph by Alamy/Photo/Brain light

Printed and bound by CPI Group (UK) Ltd, Croydon CR0 4YY
POD 2025